Why Are Castles Castle Shaped?

As a child, Philip Ardagh spent many a holiday with his parents, looking around various ruined castles dotted about Britain. It's from this that his passion for castles in particular – and history and archaeology in general – grew.

As well as having written over fifty non-fiction books, Philip Ardagh is also the author of the best-selling and very silly Eddie Dickens novels, also published by Faber & Faber, described by the *Guardian* as being a 'scrumptious cross between Monty Python and Dickens'.

Philip Ardagh currently lives with his wife, Dr Heloise Coffey, an academic, and their two (not-so-academic) cats on the south east coast of England.

WHY ARE
CASTLES
CASTLE–SHAPED?

100½

QUESTIONS ABOUT
CASTLES ANSWERED

PHILIP ARDAGH

ILLUSTRATED BY PETER GREGORY
CARTOONS BY MARK DAVIS

faber and faber

First published in 2002
by Faber and Faber Limited
3 Queen Square, London WC1N 3AU

Designed by Mackerel
Printed in Italy

A CIP record for this book
is available from the British Library

ISBN 0-571-21437-1

2 4 6 8 10 9 7 5 3 1

CONTENTS

Any complicated words and phrases are explained
in the Glossary.

Respectfully dedicated to Tove Jansson,
creator of the Moomin stories, who died (aged 86)
whilst I was compiling this book.

PLAN OF ATTACK

Questions! Questions! Questions!

There are so many questions to ask about castles and the people who lived and worked in them that it's difficult to know where to start.

The truth be told, this book has been designed for you to either read from start to finish, or to dip into out of interest or to look up the answer to any specific query you might have.

If you want to know something specific, the best place to start is with the index on page 128. There's also a rather useful glossary explaining castle terms, and a quick guide to the changing shape of castles over the years.

After every ten questions and answers, there's a QUICK QUIZ to see whether you've remembered what's gone before. The answers are on page 127.

A MESSAGE FROM THE AUTHOR

Writing this book has been a brilliant excuse for me to revisit many of my favourite castles and to discover the delights of new ones. The word 'castle' on a map can mean so many different things from a mound of earth where a castle once stood or a magnificent ruin, to someone's private home that's still lived in. They bring history to life in their own unique and exciting way.

My thanks to everyone who asked me a question. There were some great ones to choose from. Thanks also to all the staff and volunteers at all the castles I visited and who answered any questions I might have had; in particular those from English and Scottish Heritage, Cadw: Welsh Historic Monuments, the Scottish National Trust and the National Trust.

Finally, thanks as always to my editor Suzy Jenvey, who lets me write the books I want to write, which makes her worth a knight's ransom.

PHILIP ARDAGH
EAST SUSSEX
2002

1 'Who built castles?'

Rich people, usually with titles. In other words, more often than not, medieval castles were built by kings, princes, lords and knights. To build a castle, you needed money, manpower, authority and, usually, the permission of your king or overlord. Of course, these nobles – as posh people were called – didn't do the actual building work themselves. That's where the manpower part came in. They had serfs (with an 'e', rather than the kind you go surfing in) doing the basic labouring, with craftsmen carrying out the more specialised roles.

In overall charge was the architect and under him was the master mason. The master mason had a team of roughmasons, who built the walls, and freemasons, who carved the stone, which was a much more skilled job. There were also smiths to do the metalwork (the grills, portcullis, etc.) and a team of carpenters to put in wooden doors and floors. Serfs were unpaid peasants who 'belonged' to the noblemen and worked for them in return for food, land and protection in times of trouble. This was all a part of the feudal system, which you can read about in answer to Question 72.

2 'Why build castles? What were they for?'

To impress, to cause fear, to defend and to protect. A huge castle on top of high ground (and most castles are built on hills) sent out a clear message to all who saw it that this was the home of their boss and that he should be obeyed. If he was a kind boss, that was reassuring. If he was a cruel one, then that might instil you with fear.

The next biggest building for miles around was probably the village church, and that was tiny by comparison. There may be a monastery in the neighbourhood but that was full of peaceful monks. Everyone knew that a castle was bristling with soldiers, including the cavalry (knights on horseback, that is) and the latest weapons of war.

There was a time when castles and religious buildings were about the only places built from stone.

In times of trouble, people who lived in the nearby village would gather their meagre belongings and hurry to the castle, to be protected inside its high stone walls. Some experts believe that the most important function of a castle was as a safe place for horses. In the days when the fastest form of transport on dry land was a good horse, and the most feared sight was a group of knights on horseback, charging at you full tilt, it was important to keep them in the safest place possible, and a castle really fitted the bill.

3 'Why are castles up on hilltops?'

To see and to be seen. A high vantage point is very useful in war time because you can see the enemy coming. A sentry on lookout duty at the top of a tower in a castle on top of a hill could see for miles around. This made it very hard for any would-be attackers to have the element of surprise on their side. Not only that, the attackers had to trudge up hill with all their weapons and supplies, which must have made things even more tiring for them. Then there's the whole business of the castle simply looking impressive. The local serfs would, literally, look up at a huge, imposing stone building on their local hillside and be reminded of their place in society, under their lord and master who lived there. (Not all castles were built on hills, though.)

4 'Was it only important people who got to live in castles?'

No. In answer to Question 2, I said that, in times

of trouble, whole villages could seek protection within the walls of their local castle. What I didn't mention is that, on some occasions, they probably brought all their livestock — sheep, cattle, goats and chickens! — too. But, even in peacetime, the noblemen and women were in the minority within the castle walls. This wasn't out of an act of kindness but because, if you were important enough to own a castle, you were important enough to have other people do absolutely everything for you. A typical castle might include:

The Nobles

The lord and lady of the castle and their children

The lady's ladies-in-waiting

Knights loyal to his lordship (and their lady wives)

Squires, training to be knights

Pages training to be squires

Others

Chief steward, in charge of the entire household and estates

Constable, in charge of overall castle safety and security

Sergeant at arms/Captain of the guard

Stewards

Foot soldiers/guards (numerous)

Armourer

Blacksmith

Farrier (cared for the horses)

Falconer (cared for the hunting birds)

Kitchen servants

General servants

Gardeners

Kennel boy (cared for hunting dogs)

...and so on and so on. A castle was less like a house and more like a mini-community. An important role was as a garrison (barracks) for soldiers, ready to put down local rebellions and generally keep law and order in the neighbourhood.

5 'Where did everyone get to sleep?'

This, of course, depended on the type of castle you lived in. Castle design changed over time (see *The Changing Shape of Castles* on pages 116 to 119). Having said that, most castles had a great hall. Unlike in a monastery, where monks who didn't sleep in separate cells had big dormitories, there were no rooms put aside solely as 'staff quarters'. Only the noblemen and women of the castles had their own private bed chambers, on the floors above.

With a few noticeable exceptions, such as the kennel boy who'd sleep in the kennel with the hunting dogs, most servants slept together in the great hall; the same room used for big banquets and important gatherings. Although not the most comfortable place to sleep, at least this was usually directly above the kitchens, in the days when a castle's main building was the keep.

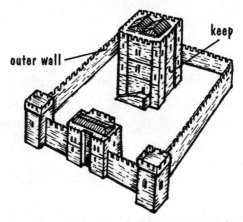

The keep (which is often the only part which remains of some castles because it was the most solid and also the hardest part for humans, time and nature to destroy) was surrounded by outer walls, some of which had buildings built into them or built up against them.

At one time there was a fashion for building kitchens in these outbuildings, because there were so many accidental fires. The advantage of having your kitchen in the keep was not only that the food was hotter when it reached you but also, in the days before central heating, a big kitchen generated a great deal of heat... which was great if you had to sleep on the floor above.

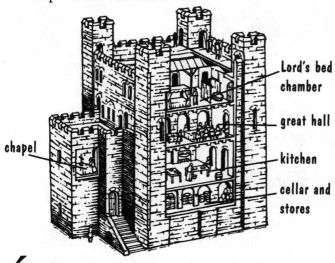

Lord's bed chamber

great hall

chapel

kitchen

cellar and stores

6 'What's a 'motte and bailey'?'

In the days before grand stone castles, the easiest way to build a castle was to dig a ditch, using the soil to create a big mound of earth called a motte. You could then build a wooden castle keep on top. Below the mound, but still surrounded by the defensive ditch, was a large courtyard called the bailey. Mottes have little to do with moats!

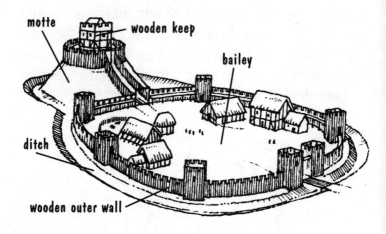

7 'Why don't all castles have moats?'

Well, to answer that, I think I should start off by explaining what a moat is to anyone who doesn't already know. It's a deep channel of water running all the way around a castle as an added form of defence. It makes it all the more difficult for a would-be attacker to get right up to the castle walls, and virtually impossible for anyone planning to tunnel their way in. (The idea of a tunnel was to make the wall above it collapse. This was called 'undermining'.)

Three very useful tools for attackers were: battering rams, for beating against a castle's doors until they were bashed in; long ladders for a soldier to lean against the side of a castle's wall, run up and jump over the top, sword in hand (a dangerous job in the heat of battle, but some poor mugs were ordered to do it) and siege towers. (You can find out more about these last ones in the answer to Question 36.)

All three of these were useless when a castle had a moat. You couldn't get your battering ram, ladder or siege tower anywhere near the outer walls of the castle you were attacking, because there was this deep channel of water between you and it. Even if you could find a way of draining the moat (and it was often fed by a stream), you'd still be left with a deep, muddy channel.

So why didn't all castles have such a useful form of protection? The answer is threefold. Firstly, some castles were built in areas without a sufficient water supply – though just about every castle had a well, because some form of water supply was vital when choosing a spot to build a castle in the first place. Secondly, the local geology had some say in whether you could dig a moat, or whether it could hold water. Digging a moat in solid rock was a waste of time. And digging a moat where the water would simply seep away was another fool's errand.

The third reason for not having a moat was the most positive one: their being no need for one. Some castles, such as the one in Edinburgh, Scotland, for example, were built on such high and impregnable rocky outcrops, that – even if somehow possible – having a moat as well would have seemed totally unnecessary!

8 'Did people keep fish in the moat?'

Moated castles (or castle ruins) that still stand today often have fish in the moat, which are an added attraction to visitors. That certainly wouldn't have been the case when the castles were built. There were often fishponds, but these were used as a source of food – a kind of 'living larder' – rather than something nice to look at.

Back then, moats were often used as rubbish tips. Worse than that, they were used as open sewers. When you went to the loo, that's often where the result ended up. The water in most moats would have been too polluted for fish to live in...

...and even more unpleasant for the poor old enemy to try to cross!

9 'Where did the people who didn't live in castles live?'

Most people were serfs (peasants) who 'worked the land'. They didn't own it, but worked on it for their lord and master in the castle. They lived in nearby villages, usually in very basic timber-framed houses. Later, when towns grew up outside castle walls, merchants (the richer 'middle class' between noblemen and women and peasants) lived in finer houses but still, usually, timber-framed ones.

10 'Were peasants' cottages really built out of animal poo?'

Yes and no! Timber-framed houses had the space between the timbers (the basic frame of the house – often just one big room) filled with something called 'wattle and daub'. The wattle was simply woven twigs. The daub was often horsehair, mud and... er... dung (which is a polite word for animal poo).

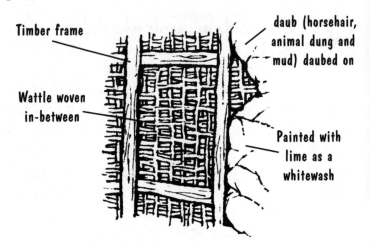

Timber frame

daub (horsehair, animal dung and mud) daubed on

Wattle woven in-between

Painted with lime as a whitewash

Quick Quiz 1

1. What was the freemason's job when building a castle?
2. Who looked after a castle's horses?
3. Give two reasons why not all castles have moats.
4. What is a garrison?
5. What is wattle?

11 'Why do so many castles have those silly slitty windows?'

They may look silly to you, but they had a very different function to windows in houses today. The main function of a window in a house is to let in light. Its secondary purpose is so that you can look outside at the 'pretty view' or to see what the weather's like, or who it is coming up the path to the front door. The function of these slitted castle windows (called arrow loops) was to be able to fire arrows out of them, whilst making it very difficult for the enemy, down below, to fire arrows back *in* through them.

It was easy enough for an archer to fire an arrow through the slit from up there inside the castle, but took much more skill for an attacker to aim an arrow into the narrow slot to kill one of the castle's archers. These weren't 'silly slitty windows', they were brilliant pieces of design!

12 'Why were so many windows cross-shaped?'

Because of the two different types of bow that the archers were using to fire arrows onto the enemy. The longbow, which made use of the upright slit of the 'cross', and the crossbow, which used the sideways slit. Both were very effective weapons in their own way.

An arrow fired from a longbow could travel much further than one from a crossbow, so could hit someone further away, but it travelled much slower. This meant that the arrow wouldn't penetrate (go in) as far as one from a crossbow. Over a shorter range, the crossbow was deadly. The arrow, known as a bolt, travelled at very high speeds and, if you were unlucky enough to get in the way, could even pass most of the way through you!

A longbow was a basic 'bow and arrow', but much larger. A skilled longbowman could fire twelve arrows in the time it took for a crossbowman to fire a single shot.

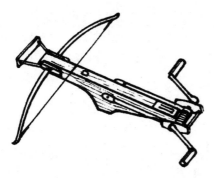

The crossbow was a much more complicated weapon. The string to the bow, often made of metal, had to be pulled so tight that it was winched into place. When released, the energy fired the bolt at impressive speeds.

13 'Didn't any castle windows have glass in them?'

With the exception of a castle's chapel window, which sometimes contained stained glass, very few – if any – medieval castles' windows had glass in them. Glass was extremely expensive and, anyway, many so-called windows were actually designed for firing arrows through. Some windows did include iron grills, to stop people falling out or climbing in, and had wooden shutters or oiled linen on the inside, to keep out the wind and the rain, though the linen could make rooms very dark and gloomy. By the time of Henry VIII, glass was being introduced, in small panes held together by lead.

Technology didn't exist for making big sheets of glass. As time went on and castles were built more for show than for battle, bigger windows were introduced, even on the outer walls and glass added.

14 'Why are some castle windows curved and others pointy?'

Probably because they were built at different times. A window or doorway with a curved arch is easier to make than one with a pointed arch. As building skills and technology got better over time, the stonemasons found they could create arches with more elaborate curves. Pointed arches are called 'gothic' arches, but there are many different kinds.

A Norman arch with ornate carving   **An early gothic arch**

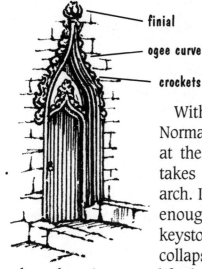

finial

ogee curve

crockets

A more ornate gothic arch in the later decorative style

With a simple curved Norman arch, the keystone at the top – put in last – takes the weight of the arch. If anyone was foolish enough to remove the keystone, the arch would collapse. With gothic arches, there is no need for keystones.

Although arches are a good way of trying to date a castle, it's important to remember that a very old castle (which started out with Norman arches) could have had newer – gothic – arches added at a later date. Also, in the 19th century a number of fake gothic castles were built which had more to do with looking good than following the strict historical rules of architecture.

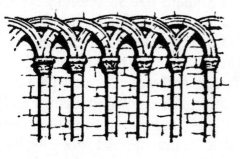

This blind arcade (row) of intercutting Norman arches gives the appearance of pointed ones.

15 'What is blind arcading?'

What, at first, appears to be blocked-in rows of arches. In fact, although windows and doorways in castles did often get deliberately walled in as use of rooms changed in castles over the centuries, blind arcading was always meant to be 'blind' (in other words, you couldn't see through it). It was there for decoration only. It's more common in monasteries and churches built for the glory of God than in castles built for defence. However, over time, castles did get more and more decorated (to show off their owners' wealth, taste and power).

16 'How did people in castles keep warm?'

With glassless windows and bare stone floors, that's a very good question! In medieval Europe, there was no such thing as central heating, even though the ancient Romans had successfully come up with such a heating system thousands of years before! Apart from plenty of layers of clothes, the heat from the kitchen, and roaring fires in their apartments, noblemen and women's two greatest weapons against the cold were wall-hangings and four-poster beds. Wall-hangings were used to keep out draughts and to warm up cold stone walls.

Four-poster beds were like a room within a room. As well as the mattress beneath you and the bedclothes over you, there was a canopy forming a roof above you, and curtains to pull all the way around. Dried rushes were strewn on the cold, bare floors.

17 'Were there flaming torches everywhere?'

Not as many as you might think if you've seen a lot of horror films with torch-lined passages leading to deep, mysterious dungeons. The truth be told, one of the *last* places a baron would waste his valuable light on was a dungeon. Let the prisoners languish in the dingy dark! (Important prisoners were kept in rich apartments and held to ransom anyway, not put in those dark smelly places. See the answer to Question 87.)

The main source of light in a castle was daylight. In medieval times, most people went to bed when it got dark. Unlike today, where electricity means we can have 24 hour light and ignore what time of day it is, much of what people used to do was dictated by daylight hours. Having said that, a roaring fire in the great hall gave off plenty of light on a dark evening, and those lucky enough to afford them could have plenty of candles. The two main types were beeswax and tallow.

Candles made from beeswax (used by bees to make their honeycomb) were much more expensive. Tallow is a mixture of animal fat and was in plentiful supply.

18 'What did they do in the evening without computer games and telly?'

The peasants went to bed soon after dark, tired after a long day's work on the land and ready to get up at first light the next morning for another hard day's slog. Guards took it in turn to keep watch from the castle battlements and gatehouses. Servants, pageboys and squires ran around making sure that the lords, ladies and knights were happy. And the lords, ladies and knights? Well, as well as enjoying a good banquet some nights (see the answer to Question 51), they might be kept amused by live-in entertainers such as dancers, jugglers and a minstrel (who sang the latest songs whilst playing a stringed instrument called the lute). There were no such things as guitars back then. (The other kind of lute, of the 'loot' variety, means stolen goods!)

The castle might also be visited by bards (poets and storytellers) and troubadours who wandered from place to place, earning their living by performing to the different lords and ladies.

19 'Did most castles really have lots of secret passages?'

Many of the larger castles were a warren of similar-looking stone corridors and those who lived and worked there probably knew some sneaky short-cuts that a visitor would never have dreamt of. Many also contained secret rooms or, at the very least, hid their doors behind wall-hangings. Having said that, there were probably never as many secret doors and passages as you may imagine... especially not behind revolving bookcases (as you often see in films). Books were all handwritten, extremely rare and most of them were kept in monasteries. No one would have had a wall full of books, let alone risk them swinging open and shut to reveal a passageway!

Having said that, there were sometimes passages known to those who lived in the castle but not necessarily those in the nearby towns or villages.

Although the City of Nottingham's medieval castle no longer exists and has a manor house (museum) on the site, the passages dug into the hill underneath, leading down to the ground, are still there! You can even see places carved into the stone to store cannon balls.

20 'Isn't there some trick about the direction stairs spiral in a castle's spiral staircase?'

Yes. It's brilliantly simple and it shows how carefully planned castles were when they were built. A spiral staircase is a staircase with a central column around which the steps spiral, a bit like a corkscrew. (In castles, they're made of stone.) They're very handy because they take up very little room, which is why they're ideal for using as stairs in castle towers, where there's no way you could fit an ordinary staircase.

The trick about most spiral staircases in castles has to do with the fact that most people are right handed. They're usually built so that if you're a knight rushing down the stairs to defend your castle, the central column is on your left and your right hand is free and clear to hack away with your sword.

The enemy attacking and trying to get up the staircase, however, finds that the central column is in the way of the swords in their right hands, making life much harder!

Quick Quiz 2

1 What are the 'slitty' glassless windows that arrows are fired through called?

2 Which can be fired further? A longbow arrow or a crossbow bolt?

3 What is a finial?

4 How can you tell a Norman and a gothic arch apart?

21 'What's the difference between a baron and a lord?'

All barons are lords, but not all lords are barons. Dukes and earls are also lords, but they're higher up the hierarchy (more senior) in the feudal system. (See Question 72.) To add to the confusion, the time came that, when a squire became a knight, he was given some land and some serfs to work on it. The knight – a 'sir' – would then be called the 'lord of the manor', even though he wasn't a Lord Somebody but a Sir Somebody! (Nobody said that life was straightforward in castle times!)

22 'How could you get to be a knight?'

To start with, you needed two things which you had no control over. You needed to be born a boy and with noble blood (in other words, to be the son of nobility). If you were lucky, you'd then go to your local castle, when you were about nine years old, and live and work there as a page, training to be a squire and then, perhaps, to be a knight.

23 'What did pageboys have to do?'

Pages spent much of their time waiting on others. They'd serve and clear food on the 'top table' in the great hall, running up and down the stairs to the kitchens with dish after dish, course after course. It was an honour to get to serve your lord and master... as well as being exhausting! They'd look after squires' horses too, as well as being taught simple sums and, in later medieval times, how to read and write. Originally, it was thought there was little reason to be literate! They could pay or order people to do that for them. Later, it became an essential part of being a true knight. Finally, there was training in horsemanship and use of weapons.

24 'Who trained all these wannabe knights and how?'

Pages and squires – one grew into the other if training went well – were often taught by older knights too old to fight any more. Training included everything from practising archery with a target, riding between posts and charging with a lance against a quintain. A squire would also be responsible for his knight's armour, weapons and horse. A squire would not only keep his knight's sword sharp and his armour clean, he'd also help him dress in the morning.

25 'What's a quintain?'

Another variation on this question is 'what do you call that thing people charge at that swings around and knocks them off their horse if they're not careful?' You call that thing a quintain! It was designed to make pages and squires into fine jousting knights. A quintain had a shield on one side and a weight on the other. The rider had to hit the shield with the tip of his lance, but avoid the weight as it then swung around, potentially knocking him off his mount!

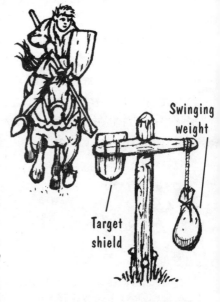

Swinging weight

Target shield

It took real skill to hit the shield and avoid the weight whilst riding fast and holding a heavy lance.

26 'What's the difference between a joust and a tournament?'

A joust was simply a part of a tournament, though it's usually the highlight. A tournament was a cross between a fair, a fête and a number of jousts, or mock battles. Usually held just outside a castle's walls, on a field called 'the lists', a typical tournament would have covered wooden seats for noble spectators, a grandstand for the lord and lady of the castle and the most distinguished guests, and plenty of brightly coloured striped tents, where knights could change in and out of their armour and people could buy everything from ale to pies. As well as all the official attractions, a tournament would attract travelling entertainers hoping to make a little money from the crowd: jugglers, fire-eaters, men with dancing bears and the like. It would also attract the occasional pickpocket and those speaking out against the dangers of the joust.

27 'Weren't jousts just knights charging at each other with lances?'

Though that alone would be impressive enough, there was a lot more to it than that. Tournaments originally started out as mock battles with whole groups of knights facing each other and fighting.

Although these were supposed to be 'friendly' and not a fight to the death, people did end up getting hurt and, sometimes, killed. As time went on, more and more rules were introduced. In the end, a pair of knights would face each other, in special armour, on horseback. Both armed with a wooden lance, they would attempt to knock the other from his mount. Once done, they might then fight on foot, with a shield and a morning star. During such encounters, they would wear their coat of arms or that of their lord. Sometimes they'd also wear a lady's 'favour' to show that they were fighting on her behalf.

This weapon is often mistakenly called a mace. It is, in fact, a morning star and could do serious damage to a knight's helmet, if not his head inside it.

Why are castles castle-shaped?

28 'What's a lady's favour?'

In the age of chivalry – and you can find out more about that in the answer to Question 63 – knights did daring deeds and fought jousts in the name of their particular ladies. If he won, he might dedicate his victory to her. To show whose 'favour he was currying', he might wear a scarf or token she had given him – tied around his arm or tucked into his gauntlet – displaying her colour or motif for all to see. Some knights, from the old way of doing things, thought this kind of thing was 'unmanly' and shouldn't be encouraged!

29 'What's a coat of arms?'

What may seem strange about an original coat of arms was that it was a coat but it didn't have any arms! No, that's not strictly true. It didn't have any sleeves. It did have 'arms' in the sense that we're talking about here.

In the days before uniforms, one knight looked pretty much like another. If kitted out from head to toe in armour, when a knight had the visor of his helmet down, it was hard to tell whether he was your local friendly neighbourhood knight... or your worst enemy. A way round this was to wear a sleeveless 'coat of arms' over your breastplate. This showed the family emblems of either the knight's own family, or the family of the lord for whom he was fighting. That way, you'd know whose side he was on.

This not only meant that his own soldiers knew who he was from a distance and whether to follow him, but had other important uses too. If killed in battle, it was often possible to identify knights by their coats of arms. Strangely, though, more often than not, it also offered a knight added protection against the enemy. His coat of arms would show that he was from a wealthy family and worth capturing rather than killing. What use was a dead knight when a live one could be held to ransom? (In other words, taken prisoner until a payment – usually a large one – is made.)

As time passed, knights simply had the emblem painted on their shield, and the shield shape, containing the various emblems, came to be called the coat of arms instead.

Like all things knightly, there were rules about what one could put on a coat of arms, and different symbols had very particular meanings. The study of coats of arms is called heraldry.

A coat of arms is divided into various sections,
each with its own special name.

THE CREST

THE HELMET or
HELM

THE SHIELD or
ESCUTCHEON

THE MOTTO
(once a battle cry)

THE SUPPORTERS
(either side)

CONCILIO ET LABORE

It would be the part within the shield, or escutcheon, that
would appear on a knight's shield.

PRECISION AND TOLERANCE

Some coats of arms contain visual puns. This 20th century coat of arms belonged to Lord Kings Norton, Baron of Wooton Underwood. The reason why the supporters are 'cocks on rocks' is because his family name was ROXBEE COX, which sounds like 'Rocks-Bee-Cocks'. For reasons of heraldry, he wasn't allowed bees on his coat of arms, which would have completed the visual joke. Instead, he had to make do with two flying gas turbine engines! This isn't so crazy when you know that Lord Kings Norton played an important role in the development of the jet engine.

30 'Did you win medals at jousts or cash prizes?'

I never won either. I was far too young! That was a... er... joke, okay? There *were* prizes, but they weren't medals and they weren't valuable. It was more the honour of taking part... and, more often than not, the winner did get offered the loser's armour. This was a big deal because, apart from his horse, armour was probably a knight's most valuable possession. The winner could keep it (out of spite, because it probably wouldn't fit him anyway) or he could sell it straight back to the loser, which was what usually happened. If the knights were friends, the armour might be bought back very cheaply. If not, it might cost a tidy sum. Some knights actually made their living in this manner, travelling from tournament to tournament, entering jousts. Despite the rules, and a marshal being there to see fair play, people were still badly injured and, occasionally killed. Jousting was certainly dangerous sport!

Did you know?

Jousting became such a spectacle that some knights wore amazing helmets with huge crests of sword-wielding men or enormous castles. If these had been made of metal, they'd have been so heavy that they'd have broken the knights' necks. The crests were, in fact, made of light wood or papier-mâché, just for show and certainly **NOT** for use in real battles!

You can find out much more about knights in the answers to Questions 61 to 70.

Quick Quiz 3

1. What were the two most important things you needed to be to have the chance of becoming a page?

2. How many 'supporters' did a typical coat of arms have?

3. Did the winner of a joust usually win the loser's

   (a) estate, (b) armour or (c) horse?

31 'What are crenelations?'

They're simply another name for the battlements. The sticking up pieces of stone are called merlons and the gaps in-between are called crenels. In later years, one had to get permission from the king before adding battlements to your home, or before building a castle. (This was just in case he thought you were building up defences against him.) Such permission was called 'a licence to crenelate'.

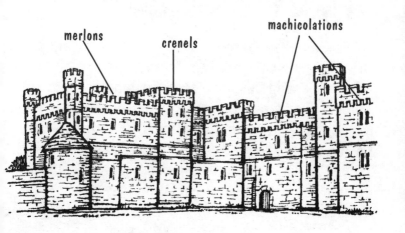

merlons   crenels   machicolations

32 'Was boiling oil really poured on unwelcome visitors?'

Just below the battlements are machicolations. These are like open-topped archways through which soldiers on the battlements could pour a whole variety of unpleasant things onto the people below. Should the enemy actually make it into the area between the portcullis and the main door, there were a whole host of other 'murder holes' through which things could be dropped on them. Although boiling oil was an option, it would have been a bit of a waste. People were far more likely to throw rocks and other painful missiles... or even the contents of their master's and mistress's chamber pots!

33 'What was a portcullis for?'

This was a spiked metal gate – more of a giant grill really – which could be dropped at a moment's notice, giving the guards more time to shut the proper wooden doors. As well as helping to keep people out, the portcullis could be dropped once some of the enemy were *in* the gatehouse, trapping them between it and the wooden doors. Then they could have things dropped on them from the murder holes!

34 'Will you draw us a drawbridge?'

Ho! Ho! This question was obviously asked by someone who doesn't know about my drawing skills... or the distinct lack of them! I leave that to the professionals! The first mechanical drawbridges were raised and lowered with ropes or chains attached to the part of the bridge that went across the ditch or moat (see the cover of this book, for example). Later, they became much more sophisticated,with the mechanism safely protected inside the castle gatehouse, such as the one below.

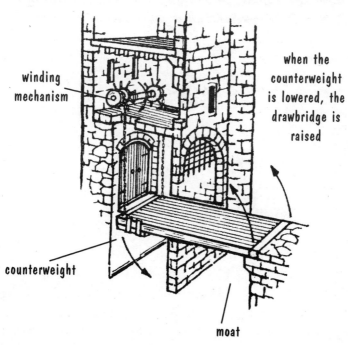

winding mechanism

when the counterweight is lowered, the drawbridge is raised

counterweight

moat

Many castles had a long, fixed bridge leading to a tower on an island in the moat called the barbican (the tower that is, not the island). There would then be a drawbridge leading from the barbican, across a further stretch of the moat, to the castle gatehouse, where it could be raised and lowered. Rather than lining up with the barbican and drawbridge, the fixed bridge was at right-angles to it, running parallel with the castle's outer wall. Why? So that the castle's archers had an easy target as the enemy rode along it. When it came to building castles, everything was done for a good reason.

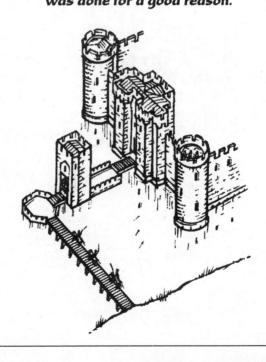

35 'What was a castle siege?'

When an attacking army tried to stop anyone going in or coming out. Sometimes this was the only way to win a castle. If the castle was built in the right place with all the right defences and even had a moat preventing tunnelling, there was no way an army could attack it. The people inside the castle had all the advantages... for the time being. But imagine what would happen if no one could get in or out. There would be no fresh supplies of food or arrows, or even reinforcements. Once you'd eaten the last of the supplies and the horses and the rats and decided not to eat the others who'd already died of starvation and disease, what could you do? When the enemy army outside wanted new food they could send for it. When they grew tired after firing a few catapults, they could call up fresh soldiers... but not those trapped in the castle.

The only way a siege could end with the castle victorious would be if the occupants held out so long that the attacking army, which had been laying siege, simply gave up and went away (which was unlikely) or help came in the form of reinforcements from elsewhere, attacking the enemy outside. It's through successful sieges that some of the most impregnable castles have been won.

36 'What was a siege tower?'

It's not a part of a castle, which you might expect. It was actually a large wooden tower – sometimes called a belfry – with various floors reached by ladders on the inside. If there was no moat around the castle, the tower could be wheeled up against the wall and, from the safety of within the tower, the attackers could climb up to the height of the top of the wall and jump out over the battlements. The best way of trying to stop this was by trying to set fire to the wooden structure. The first siege towers appeared in ancient Roman times.

37 'Did attackers really use giant catapults?'

Indeed they did. They did indeed. Not the big Y-shaped ones with a piece of elastic across the top, but huge wooden affairs with a firing arm that was pulled back on ropes and then released. There were two main types. The ordinary catapult with a fixed firing arm (where you put your large boulder or dead horse) and the slingshot catapult, with a loose sling (to put your rock in) at the end of the arm. Like the siege tower in the previous answer, both of these giant catapults owe much to Roman design.

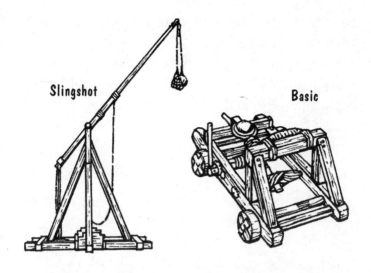

Slingshot

Basic

**Shots fired from catapults were meant to damage people,
not the castle itself.**

38 'What were you supposed to batter with a battering ram?'

Well, it wouldn't be much good battering a stone wall, and the wooden shutters on windows were rather too high up to have a go at, so the obvious answer is the wooden doors. Of course, with the drawbridge up, that acts like an additional door. If the attacking army could make their own makeshift bridge across to the closed drawbridge, then the battering ram could have a go at that too.

The first battering rams were probably simply logs cut down in a nearby forest when needed.

Over time, they became more sophisticated. Rather than men having to carry them as they charged at a gate, battering rams were mounted on wheels, with a canopy above it. The canopy was to protect both the ram and the people wheeling it from attack from above.

39 'When did people start using cannons?'

The thing which fired the cannonball out of the cannon was gunpowder. When lit, it caused an explosion which shot the ball out of the end and into the air. The Chinese had discovered how to make gunpowder – mixing potassium nitrate with charcoal and sulphur – in the early 11th century. Their earliest written record of the formula dates back to 1045 (21 years before William the Conqueror invaded England and the first Norman castles were built on English soil). The thing was, though, that the Chinese were using it to make firecrackers, not war! By 1232, though, there are Chinese records of using gunpowder to make 'war rockets', whatever they may have been!

It wasn't until the early 14th century that the secret of gunpowder had reached Europe. By 1340, it was being produced in England on a large scale. And what was it first used for? To fire huge balls (the size of big pumpkins) from the first – very basic – cannons which were called bombards.

Bombards are very significant in the history of the castle, because they mark the beginning of the end. They were really the first weapon specifically designed to do serious damage to the structure of the castle itself, and not just the people in it. The ball from a bombard could knock a hole through a castle wall. Once cannons and firearms improved, this marked the beginning of the end of knights in armour (they could be shot) and existing castles as strongholds. Buildings needed a rethink in design.

40 'Didn't anyone have guns?'

In medieval times? Yes. In the 1320s, a few guns had been tried out in Europe, but to pretty disastrous effects. The problem was igniting – lighting – the gunpowder. More often than not, it was the person firing the gun who was injured (sometimes horribly) rather than the person they were shooting at... so the idea didn't catch on until the technology had developed. It wasn't until the late 16th century that the flintlock method of igniting the gunpowder was invented, and the rifle became a really useful weapon in a soldier's armoury.

After the invention of handguns –
usually primitive rifles – arrow loops (see
Question 11) were replaced with gun loops, for
sticking the barrel out through the castle wall
and firing on your
enemy. The first gun
loops were simply round
holes, so the soldier
couldn't see where he
was aiming. Later came
the oilet, a gun loop (or
gun port) with an
additional upright slit
for the soldier to take
aim through.

An OILET gun loop

Look
through
here

Fire
through
here

Quick Quiz 4

1. What was the royal
   permission to add battlements
   to your property called?
2. Why did fixed bridges often
   run parallel to a castle's wall
   instead of cutting straight
   across the moat to the drawbridge?
3. What is a belfry?
4. Name the earliest
   type of cannon.

41 'Did castles have loos?'

Yes. Although lords and ladies sometimes used pots in their chambers (which came to be called chamber pots), there were small rooms set aside to use as loos. There was no plumbing or flushing. Unlike in the case of the chamber pots, which servants emptied, cleaned out and returned – what a fun job that must have been – there were no pots in these rooms. Called garderobes, they contained a seat with a hole in it. These holes were above stone chutes set into the outer walls, or simply overhung them. The resulting waste usually fell into the moat, making it an even less desirable place for the enemy to swim across. The stench must have been dreadful in some instances. My know-all editor, Suzy, tells me that public loos in Italy are still called 'garderobes' to this day. Who am I to doubt her?

42 'Did they have toilet paper?'

Not especially made for the purpose, though they

did sometimes use old, unwanted parchment and large leaves. Herbs were sometimes left in the garderobe to make it more sweet smelling; an early form of pot pourri (a basic air-freshener).

43 'Did they have baths?'

If you mean did they have bathrooms and bath tubs, the answer is no. If you mean 'did they ever bathe?' the answer is also no... or, to be fair, very rarely! In the days before anyone knew about germs, and there was no hot and cold running water, Europeans rarely saw the point of baths. It was only after the Crusades that people came back with ideas of washing, learnt from the Arabs. Though bathing might have been a little more common after that, it wasn't a regular event. There are stories about noblemen having baths twice a year 'whether they needed them or not'. Soap too was an idea brought back from the Crusades.

44 'What were the Crusades all about?'

They were wars fought between Christians from Western Europe and Muslims, from 1096 until 1291, which was a period of just five or six years under 200! The Christians wanted control over what was called the Holy Land. (Today, this is made up of Israel and Israeli-occupied territories.) The Seljuk Turkish Muslims wanted to keep it for themselves. The main place of interest was the holy city of Jerusalem. There were eight Crusades in all, with control over Jerusalem changing a number of times. Although religious in origin, the Europeans probably used the war as an excuse to try to grab more land and riches. Europeans returned home with many ideas and discoveries they'd got from the Muslims, such as the soap I've already mentioned.

Did you know?

In the year 2000, Pope John Paul II (head of the Catholic Church) made a historic speech in the city of Jerusalem, apologising to Muslims and Jews for the death and terrible destruction caused by Christian Crusaders in the holy wars of long ago.

45 'What new discoveries did the Crusaders bring back with them?'

Perfumes and spices they'd never seen or smelt before. A wonderfully soft and shimmering fabric made from the thread of a silk worm called – you guessed it – silk. Carpets and rugs handmade to incredibly high standards, like nothing seen at home. And amazing medical advances too. (Something the Europeans didn't learn from the Arabs was that our blood is pumped around the body. That wasn't discovered in the West until William Harvey made the discovery in 1615!) They did, however, teach Europeans the importance of things such as poultices, a form of medicated bandage to put on a wound.

46 'Were there doctors around in castle times?'

Arab doctors were far more like 'proper' doctors than those in Western Europe in medieval times. Apothecaries were chemists who mixed their little knowledge of herbs with a pinch of magic and plenty of wishful thinking that their cures might work. Much of what we think of as science and medicine today was borne out of the half-science, half-hocus pocus work of earlier centuries. Genuine advances were made by trial and error, along with the dedication of a few good men and women. Some monks became adept at choosing the right herbs to help soothe particular aches, pains and maladies. Some castles had well-stocked herb gardens too.

Because he was used to mixing potions of exact amounts, it was often the job of the apothecary to mix the gunpowder from a closely guarded formula (recipe). To avoid dangerous sparks – which might blow up both him and the precious gunpowder – he would dampen the mixture with vinegar. Water damaged gunpowder but vinegar evaporated off. Mixing gunpowder was one job *not* to be done by flickering candlelight!

47 'What's alchemy?'

Alchemy was a pseudo-science (a fake science) in which the alchemists' ultimate goal was to turn ordinary metal into gold. There were some alchemists who took their work very seriously and really thought it could be done – making some genuinely important scientific discoveries on the way – and some who were frauds and tricksters, who saw it as a way of making the best life for themselves. An important tool, sought by most alchemists in the quest to make gold, was called 'the philosopher's stone'. If that sounds familiar, it's because a certain J.K. Rowling used it in the UK title of her first Harry Potter adventure!

48 'Did Merlin really exist?'

According to legend, there was once a great and mighty king who ruled the Britons and his name was Arthur. King Arthur's most trusty aide, confidant and friend was the wizard Merlin... well, as I said, that's how the legend goes. You may be surprised to learn, though, that there's more historical evidence that Merlin existed than there is that Arthur ever did! Of course, his actually having had magical powers is another matter. He might have called himself a wizard, though, and people were understandably far more superstitious and likely to believe in magic back then.

49 'Was there really such a person as King Arthur?'

There are references to a 'King Arthur' in a Welsh poem called 'Y Gododdin' written round about the year 600. That's so long ago that it looks less like a date and more like a number. In fact, that was over 1,400 years ago. The first detailed story of King Arthur's so-called life was written by Geoffrey of Monmouth in 1139, over 500 years later, but the most famous telling of the Arthurian legend is probably Sir Thomas Malory's *Morte d'Arthur*, written even later still. This means that any so-called 'facts' appeared a long time after the event.

If King Arthur really did exist and really was a king of the Britons, it was probably a small part of Britain and at the time when the Romans were still in the country. Far from commanding knights in shining armour, he's more likely to have been commanding those in animal skins. We owe so much of our image of Arthur and his Knights of the Round Table to the Victorians' fascination for him in poetry and painting.

50 'What was supposed to be the big deal of Arthur having a round table?'

Where you sat in a great hall at meal times said a lot about how important you were. The most important table to sit at was the high table. It was raised above the others and, whilst those on lower tables ate off stale bread, those on the top table had wooden platters. The lord or king's most important guest or loyal follower sat on his right (which is where the phrase 'he's my right-hand man' comes from). The next most important would sit on his left, or next to his wife if she was seated at his side.

Salt was very expense and often displayed in a huge salt cellar (for some reason often shaped like a sailing ship) and placed in a special position on the table. If you sat on the same end of the table as the lord or king 'above the salt' then you were considered far superior to those 'below the salt'. Introduce a round table and place the salt in the middle, and there is no above or below the salt. Everyone is as equal as can possibly be.

Quick Quiz 5

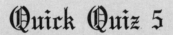

1 *What are a castle's loos called?*
2 *Where were the Crusades fought?*
3 *What were apothecaries?*

51 'Did people in castles have banquets every night?'

No, though you'd be forgiven for thinking so when watching old movies about Robin Hood or knights in shining armour. Noble families usually ate well, though. The food was always best in the summer months because storing food wasn't as easy as it is nowadays, with modern technology. Meat was stored in salt in autumn so there'd be something to serve up in the winter. All the year round, noble men and women ate fish on Fridays. Most castles had their own private fishponds, and they weren't there as something pretty to look at. When there were banquets, on special occasions, there were plenty of courses: including fish, fowl (bird) and (red) meat, with pies and vegetables. There was plenty to drink too, and the whole affair would have been very noisy indeed, with plenty of shouting and laughter. Most people sat on benches. Only the most important people had chairs.

Wine was served in hollow animal horns or metal or wooden goblets. Beer was usually served in mugs called tankards. A popular dish was roast swan. When it was served, by a page or squire, it'd had most of its feathers put back in, so it looked almost alive!

52 'Did they eat everything with their fingers?'

No! Although fingers were useful for grasping most things, they also used their knives. These weren't laid out on the table for them, like cutlery today, but would be their own knives which they carried around with them for one-hundred-and-one different uses from self-defence to cutting notches in a stick!

53 'Is it true you were supposed to throw your leftovers to the dogs?'

Yup, and it made sense when you think about it. It

meant less to clear from the tables and kept the dogs happy at the same time. The dogs in the great hall of the castle at meal times would be the master's. They'd have been a big breed and probably used for hunting.

54 'Was burping good manners?'

Very much so! A good belch was a way of showing appreciation for a meal much enjoyed... but don't go getting any bright ideas. What's considered polite changes as fast as some fashions!

55 'Could you really eat your plate?'

Yes and no. It was edible, but to eat it wasn't the polite thing to do. Rather than throw away a loaf when it went stale, it would be cut into slabs, called trenchers, and used as plates. You'd eat your meal off it and it would soak up the gravy and the juices. Then, at the end of the meal, the trencher would be given to the poor. (Yes, you guessed it: serfs.) Though they'd have probably preferred the meal you'd just had, a trencher soaked in juice would be much appreciated! Someone who enjoys their food is still said to be 'a good trencherman'. Now you know where that expression comes from.

56 'Why didn't people use forks?'

I've chosen to include this question because it's typical of a type of question. It's a perfectly good question – why not indeed – but it's one of those which could be answered 'well, because they didn't and that's that'. There are so many things we take for granted nowadays that it's difficult to imagine a time before them, but such times did exist. With manners very different than they are today, and people far less worried about dirt and unaware of germs, no one had come up with the idea of using a fork yet. That's all!

57 'Why do films about castles always show someone carrying a huge plate with a boar's head with an apple in its mouth on it?'

Well, this probably wins the award for the longest question in the book. The answer is because wild boar's head was a very popular dish in medieval times. When Christmas was celebrated, it was *the* dish to have. Part of what made it so special was that the boar had to be hunted, and the bigger the boar's head you ended up with, the bigger and fiercer the boar you had to kill to get it. The apple was in there to hold the shape of the mouth and to show off the tusks and teeth. There's even an ancient carol called *The Boar's Head Carol* and it was only when the poor old wild boar were virtually wiped out in England that people had to dream up new dishes to replace it.

58 'How did they cook without cookers?'

Castle kitchens had bread ovens, huge fires over which pots of water could be hung to boil vegetables, and in front of which huge pieces of meat could be roasted on a spit. A spit was a giant skewer on which the meat – a whole carcass in some instances – could be rotated by a kitchen hand turning a handle. Underneath the spit was a tray to catch the fat dripping from the cooking meat. Turning the spit was a very hot and tiring job.

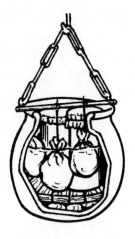

Different dishes
could be cooked
in a cauldron all
at once.

59 'Did people back then eat vegetables we don't eat now?'

I expect that there are some types of root that used to be popular then which aren't eaten now. Cooking has a lot to do with trial and error and, in times of famine, when food was scarce, I'm sure people would have tried boiling up anything and everything, particularly if they were poor. There are certainly whole varieties of fruit and vegetables that don't exist any more, even though we might be eating the same type of things.

Of course, things are really much more the other way around. With nowhere in the world more than 24 hours away, we can get to taste exotic fruit and vegetables our medieval ancestors could never have dreamed of.

Did you know?

People in medieval Europe never laid eyes on a potato. These grew wild in the Americas, which weren't discovered by the Europeans until the 15th century. Legend has it that it was Sir Walter Raleigh who brought a potato back to England in the 16th century, and presented it to Queen Elizabeth I. In fact, there's an earlier record of a potato being eaten in England. Unfortunately, the people ate the stalk and leaves (which are poisonous) and threw away the spud itself. They were very ill, so the idea of potato eating didn't instantly catch on.

 'How can beer be small?'

All castles needed a water supply, but that doesn't mean to say that anyone thought that the water was fit to drink in the state it was when it came out of the ground! Unless you were lucky enough to have built your castle right next to a sparkling spring – which might have led to constant worries about the foundations sinking anyway – more often than not, the water was muddy and brown.

It was therefore standard practice to brew as much beer as possible. Of course, to make the beer you must use the water but, by the time it had brewed, it tasted a lot better than mud and was supposed to be brown! Ordinary beer – big beer – would be drunk when you wanted a good time. If you were a child – or at a time when you'd simply have drunk the water if it wasn't so disgusting – you'd have a much weaker brew called small beer. So now you know!

Today, the phrase 'small beer' is sometimes used to describe someone or something that's thought to be of little or no consequence.

Quick Quiz 6

1 What's a trencher?
2 How was meat roasted in a castle kitchen?
3 What kind of knife did most men eat with?
4 What happened to much of the leftovers?

61 'What's a harness of armour?'

A harness of armour is simply the correct name for a suit of armour. Every single piece, from the plume of the helmet down to the tip of the toe – including ankle and knee joints – has its own special name. This harness is from 16th century England:

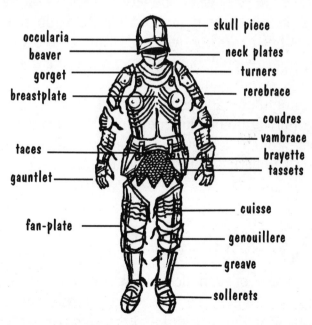

- occularia
- beaver
- gorget
- breastplate
- taces
- gauntlet
- fan-plate

- skull piece
- neck plates
- turners
- rerebrace
- coudres
- vambrace
- brayette
- tassets
- cuisse
- genouillere
- greave
- sollerets

Of course, armour was different in different countries and was forever being improved. The lighter and more flexible it became, the easier it was for the knight to move about in battle.

62 'Were knights really winched onto horses?'

I'm reluctant to say 'never' in a book, but this is as near to never as I'll get! There are no historical records of medieval knights being winched onto horses, either drawn or written. This was a fantastical idea dreamt up much later as a part of the romantic revival – a fantasy idea of what life was like in the Age of Chivalry. If a knight's armour was so heavy that he couldn't climb up onto a horse but had to be winched, think of the weight the horse would have to carry... There'd be no galloping into battle. And if the knight fell off, he'd be lying there: an easy, overweight target.

A fully armoured knight usually climbed onto his horse from a block, with the help of his squire. The more flexible and lighter armour became, the easier this was.

63 'What's chivalry?'

The code of conduct by which knights were supposed to live their lives. Being a knight was all about serving one's lord and the king. (In fact, the word 'knight' comes from the Old English word *cniht* meaning servant.) A knight was also required to be 'quick to perform honourable deeds' and to judge people 'not by their importance but their character'. Chivalry also required a knight to be loyal, generous, polite and brave.

Tied up with chivalry, there was something called 'courtly love' where a medieval knight was supposed to carry out heroic deeds in the name of a lady he 'worshipped'. Some noblemen and women found this idea particularly romantic and chivalrous... others were worried that it'd make the knights soft rather than strong, fighting men!

64 'Were some knights more senior than other knights?'

A knight was a knight was a knight, but some were from bigger or more influential and important families than others, and some were given positions of more authority than others. If you were a friend of the king you were likely to have a better 'job' and to command more respect than a knight stuck in a castle in some faraway outpost. Having said that, there weren't specific ranks within knighthood as there are in the army.

65 'What's the point of chainmail?'

The earliest armour would have been made of thick leather and the first metal armour was chainmail:

thousands of tiny loops of metal linked together to make a suit. It was incredibly flexible but not thick enough to prevent arrows and pikestaffs getting through to your flesh.

When technology advanced enough to make plates of solid metal to put together to make a whole harness of armour, chainmail was still useful for covering the gaps in the joins that were required for flexibility and movement.

The knights in the Bayeux Tapestry are shown wearing chainmail armour

66 'What weapons did the average knight have?'

As with armour, a knight's arsenal of weapons would have changed over time. You can be sure that he carried a broadsword, though. A

74

broadsword was designed for hacking a person with the side of the blade rather than stabbing them with the point (though you could give that a go).

A knight would also use a mace and a morning star. Lances were usually reserved for jousting and not the battlefield. Daggers were often worn in the belt when knights were out of their armour and in their ordinary clothes. They used them to eat with, as well as protection against surprise attack!

mace

morning star

67 'Were there really such things as armoured horses?'

In the sense that many knights' horses wore some protective armour, yes. It was his horse that gave a knight his great advantage in battle: speed, height above the foot soldiers fighting, and powerful, thunderous hooves beneath him. The horse was also the knight's weakest link. A horse up against a row of enemy foot soldiers could be poked, prodded, hacked and attacked. The better protection the horse had, the better for the knight ... but too much armour might distress the animal and slow it down. The main armour was to the head. At tournaments, the armour was as much for show as anything else and some horse armour was very ornate.

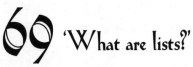 68 'What does 'hands high' mean?'

Well, it's not another way of saying 'stick 'em up!' Rather than metres or feet, horses were (and still are) measured in units called hands. In the same way that the foot measurement was originally based on the size of an average Roman soldier's foot, a hand measurement was originally based on the size of an average hand (probably an ancient Egyptian's).

The height of horses are usually measured in hands from their front hoof to their withers (the highest part of a horse's back, behind the neck between the shoulders) – you don't include the neck or head. A hand measures 10 cm (4 inches).

69 'What are lists?'

Usually the field of combat at a tournament (see

Question 26) where jousting knights came charging at each other with great big lances. The dividing fences between charging knights were called tilts.

70 'Did they really meet in stripy tents on battlefields?'

Battles used to be much more 'gentlemanly' affairs than they are today, with the opposing armies lining up neatly opposite each other before a single arrow was fired. In these instances, those lords, kings and nobles who chose not to lead their men into battle would often observe the fighting from a good vantage point up on a hill and – yes – they were sometimes housed in stripy tents.

Knights with their noble background, excellent training, expensive armour and horses were seen as a valuable asset in a battle as were the skilled archers and bowmen who could attack the enemy from a good distance. It was the poor old foot soldier – often an untrained, badly armed peasant brought off the land to fight – who was seen as 'dispensable' by his masters. In other words, they were there to make up the numbers and it didn't matter so much if they were killed or injured! (That's not my opinion, but the thinking at the time.)

Quick Quiz 7

1 What is a harness of armour?
2 What is chivalry?
3 How was chainmail made?

71 'When were most castles built?'

The main castle-building period in Europe was from the late 11th century to the early 15th century. After that, the feudal system was coming to an end and weapons technology meant that castles were no longer impenetrable (un-get-in-able) and indestructible (un-destroy-able). These were also more peaceful times.

In England, it was the 400 years after the start of the Norman Conquest (in 1066) that saw the rise and fall of castle building. That's not to say that castles simply fell into disrepair or became houses thereafter. Many took on a new lease of life in the 17th century as part of the civil war between the Cavalier royalists and the Roundhead parliamentarians led by Oliver Cromwell. In troubled Scotland, castles carried on being built right up until the 17th century anyway.

At least 84 (!!!) castles were built in Britain in the first 15 years after the Norman Conquest which is, if you're in any doubt, a staggering number. Even though William had a fairly good claim to the English throne and was now king, the Normans were really an occupying foreign power using their military might (and the feudal system) to stay in control. With Norman castles packed full of Norman lords and knights, what Anglo Saxon (the English there before them) was going to dare argue with their authority?

The Welsh proved to be a thorn in the new kings of England's sides which is why it was necessary for Edward I to build a chain of magnificent castles in Wales, over 200 years after the death of William. It was to remind the rebellious locals who was boss!

One of the most famous Norman castle keeps in Britain is often overlooked as being such because it became part of a much bigger complex of buildings, which is now a huge tourist attraction: the white tower at the Tower of London.

The Tower of London

72 'What was the feudal system?'

In the Middle Ages, how much land you had was the key to your power and wealth, and it was this land which was controlled by those in castles. The most powerful person in the land was usually the king or emperor. He gave his nobles – usually lords – land in return for their loyalty and fighting alongside him against his enemies in times of trouble. The nobles then gave some of their land to their knights who promised to fight for them. And where did the serfs – the peasants – fit into all of this? Well, for 'land' read 'land and people'. When a king gave a lord land he gave him the people living and working on it too... and when a lord gave land to a knight, the same thing happened. In other words: the king bossed the lords around, the lords bossed the knights around and EVERYONE bossed around the poor old peasants! (And, yes, before you ask, it was sometimes a queen on the throne and not a king.)

In the feudal system (sometimes referred to as 'feudalism', but it's the self-same thing) people could be divided into three main groups: people who fought, which included the king, lords, knights, guards and full-time foot soldiers; people who prayed, which included everyone from archbishops to monks; and people who worked, which included everyone from the peasants working the land to blacksmiths and merchants (though they were expected to fight too, if things got really bad).

Over time, some lords and knights did less and less actual fighting on behalf of their king. He would let them off in return for money. Also, as towns grew – still within the protection of a nearby castle – the merchants (the buyers and sellers) grew in wealth and power and became a kind of middle class. Skilled craftsmen, such as stonemasons (who were actually involved in castle-building), were also widely respected and becoming part of a middle class. Then there was the Church. One of the biggest landowners in Britain, for example, was the Church, which was, at that time, the Holy Catholic Church ruled by the pope in the Vatican in Rome. In other words, the pope had people loyal to him, not the English king, living on English soil! Religion was a hugely important part of people's everyday life.

TWO FEUDAL PYRAMIDS

king or emperor

lords and ladies
loyal to their king

knights loyal to their lords
and ladies and their king

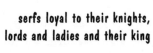

serfs loyal to their knights,
lords and ladies and their king

83

 pope

 king (supposed to be) loyal to the pope

 bishops loyal to the pope and then their king, lords and ladies loyal to their king

merchants loyal to their town's lords and ladies and their king

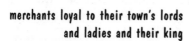

 serfs in the town loyal to their merchants, their lords and ladies and to the king

73 'Just how important was religion in castle times?'

Unbelievably. Not only were wars, such as the Crusades (see the answer to Question 44) fought over religion, but churches and cathedrals were built right across Europe, taking up enormous amounts of money, skilled labour and manpower, simply for the glory of God. Or, to be more accurate, to try and ensure that whoever was behind the project, earned a place in heaven! A nobleman would begin his day with prayer and no castle would be complete without its chapel. Prayers were even said on the battlefield.

As merchants and craftsmen (they usually had to be men) became richer and more influential they set up trade guilds. To begin with, their function was, first and foremost, to agree on trade practices – such as how long someone had to be an apprentice before they could become a professional cooper (barrel-maker) or whatever. By late medieval times, though, a guild's main function was to save up enough money to pay priests to sing masses for the souls of its dead members.

There were very few books in medieval times. There was no printing, so they had to be copied out by hand. If there was one book a castle owned, more likely than not it was a bible. Those noblemen who could write would often record their family tree in the front of their family bible – adding births, deaths and marriages as they occurred – not only because the bible was so important to them but also because it was the only book they had to hand.

Because of their religious nature, most books were copied by monks in monasteries. Sometimes rows of them would be at work, copying out text. Most books were written with quill pens, in Latin. The capital letters at the start of chapters were often very ornate, containing brightly coloured small pictures within them and sometimes even gold-leaf was applied. Pages were often given ornate borders of intricate patterns or scenes from medieval life. Such books were called illuminated manuscripts. Fortunately, some survive today and the pictures contained within the text tell us a great deal about life in medieval times. (See page 112).

74. 'If nobles were 'upper class' and serfs 'working class', who was 'middle class'?'

Although this question is kind of answered in my answer to Question 72, I think it's a good one and is worth looking at a bit more closely, because there didn't use to be a middle class: you were either born a noble or a serf... and there was little, if anything, you could do to change that. Then, over time, people not of noble birth began to get jobs which were more respected by nobles than those carried out by peasant serfs on the land.

Someone who could make beautiful jewellery or carve beautifully in stone, or bring back rare materials from faraway places, were treated as 'better people' than those digging ditches or ploughing fields. If your father was a blacksmith, you might learn the trade under him but turn your skills working with metal to making swords or armour, and earn a reputation for making particularly fine pieces. You've gone up in the world. 'Superior servants' who did more of the telling-what-to-do than the actual doing also began to be seen as middle class.

Then there are those merchants I talked about earlier. If they bought cheap and sold expensive, they were soon making good money and could afford fine clothes and houses... and higher taxes no doubt. So, unlike the 'upper class' and 'working class' – the nobles and serfs – who were the backbone of the idea of feudalism, the middle class actually grew out of feudalism: they were as a result of it.

75 'What did castle towns look like?'

I put this question here because most castle towns
were market towns, which brought in money and
made them prosperous. Barons usually had to get
permission from the king to start up a market. A
castle town usually had a castle to one side, at the
best defensive position (often still on a hill), and a
walled town spread out beside it. The wall of the
town would have battlements and towers and one
or two gatehouses, which were the only way
anyone could leave or enter the town or reach the
castle. Originally, such towns grew up around
castles. Later, they were built at the same time.
They'd include everything you'd expect in a town:
a church, homes, shops, market place, guildhalls,
etc. with the added protection of a guarded wall all

the way around it. At night the gates would be shut and the people inside would be a lot safer.

76 'Were towns safer than villages?'

Towns were very smelly, dirty places. Few houses had loos, so you used a bucket then threw the result out of the window onto the street, aiming for a ditch of open water. There were no covered drains. Towns were full of people, carts and animals being driven to market. These attracted thieves and rogues and, more likely than not, someone might try to pick your pocket. They're not the charming places that some beautifully preserved medieval towns, such as Lavenham in Suffolk, are today. Despite all of these things, towns were generally safer than villages. Villagers had the added worry of hungry wolves on the prowl in winter and thieves on the roads. Most towns had guards (acting as a kind of police force) and walled towns could actually shut out strangers at night... villages were much more vulnerable to a swift attack. As more and more houses in the richer towns began to be built with stone, the timber-framed houses of villages were also more vulnerable to fire.

77 'What's a curfew?'

At a given time each night, a bell was rung in a castle town warning that the gates were about to be shut and barred. This meant that no one could leave or enter until the following morning. This also meant that people inside the town should cover their fires (which they'd been cooking supper or warming themselves by) with a special clay pot, to avoid any fires breaking out in the town overnight. Although the term 'curfew' actually comes from the name of the pots (originally *couvrefeu*, French for 'cover fire'), 'curfew' has come to mean an official regulation restricting people's movements, usually at night.

Did you know?

Very few people knew how to read so the signs hanging outside shops had to be pictures or symbols, giving clues as to what service they offered or goods they sold. A picture of a loaf of bread meant a baker's. A giant pair of wooden scissors meant someone selling cloth to make clothes.

78 'Did clothes' fashions change much?'

Fashion – for nobles – certainly changed over time,

but not quite in the way it does today. As 'new' materials (such as silk) were brought back from abroad and technological advances were made, so clothes changed. A good example of this is armour. It always had one key purpose – you guessed it: to protect the person wearing it – but, as skills at working with metals improved, armour could be made lighter and shinier, but it was also made more ornate, or frightening-looking (to upset the enemy).

Ordinary clothes changed too, though, and some changes were new fashion for new fashion's sake, but things didn't change nearly as quickly as they do now with a 'new season's look' every few months or so! Fashion was important in the Middle Ages, though, giving lords and knights and ladies a chance to show off their wealth and style. Medieval women's hats are a great example of changing fashions:

Women's headcoverings ranged from the simple to the ridiculous.

They would wear everything from a simple headdress to the steeple hat or 'hennin'. Some hennins (supported with a wire frame inside) were over 1 metre (3 feet) tall! Colour was all-important. It was a kind of code. Blue meant that the wearer was in love.

79 'What did noble women do all day?'

I suspect that this question was borne out of the fact that, when talking about castles, it's nearly always the men who seem to do everything from building them to guarding them. Girls couldn't train to be knights. Women couldn't fight on the battlefield. What really amazes most people though, is just how few jobs there were for women in most castles. Apart from the lady of the castle, and her ladies-in-waiting (some of them wives of her husband's knights and all of noble birth), the only other women in most castles worked in the laundry. All the other jobs from bed-making to working in the kitchens were, 99 times out of 100, carried out by boys and men. So what did noble women do all day?

The lady of the castle, in other words the wife of the lord, usually played an extremely important part in castle life. She would discuss the day-to-day running of the castle with the chief steward, talking through everything from the menu of an upcoming banquet to the moving of furniture or the planting of herbs in the garden. He would then, in turn, instruct the servants. While her husband was busy organising his knights or dealing with 'matters of state' it was down to her to make sure that everything was running smoothly in the household. When the lord was away on business or off fighting, she took on even more responsibility, organising everything from more supplies from the villages to carrying out repairs to the castle itself. Hers was a very important and busy role... even though women were considered 'inferior' to men. (Let me pause here until the booing and hissing stops.)

When a noble girl was about 6 years old, it was likely that she'd be sent to *another* castle to learn how to manage the household... so each lady of the castle was training someone other than their own daughter! By the time the girl was fourteen or so, she'd usually be off their hands because she'd be married and have moved into a household of her own. (Marriages between children of royal and noble families were usually arranged when the children were still in their cradles!)

Ladies-in-waiting were companions for the lady of the castle. They helped her dress and combed her hair, ran simple errands and entertained her. They were someone for her to talk to and to share ideas with and, more often than not, became close friends. They weren't servants. They were nobles too, remember.

Noblewomen spent much of their free time at embroidery, not to be confused with tapestry. To make tapestries, you needed a wooden-framed machine called a loom. To embroider, you needed a needle. Some Victorian paintings show early medieval women with spinning wheels. This is misleading. Spinning wheels (designed to spin wool into fine thread) weren't introduced into Europe until the mid-to-late 13th century.

Other, contemporary, pictures show women by dove-cotes admiring white doves. (Some castles even had built-in dove-cotes, with holes in the stone for doves and pigeons to roost.) Although a pretty sight, this is another example of 'the living larder', such as the fish in the fishpond. The birds were there to be eaten. Noblewomen certainly enjoyed hunting with birds, though. Hawking was the sport of kings!

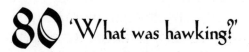 'What was hawking?'

It's another name for falconry: hunting with birds

of prey. Noblemen loved hunting. With dogs, they hunted wild boar, wolves, foxes and even bears. As well as seeing it as 'fine sport', more often than not, the animals they killed ended up as meat on the dinner table. (Peasants who tried to catch so much as a rabbit, in an area set aside for nobles' hunting, could end up paying with their lives.)

Although some women might have enjoyed hunting with dogs, falconry was seen as more ladylike. Like everything in medieval society, the type of bird you used when hawking depended on your status (your rank) in society. A lord hunted with a peregrine falcon. A lady hunted with the smaller hawk.

All the birds were looked after and trained by the castle's falconer and kept in a special wooden building – like a low, long shed – called a mews. During a hunt, the bird would sit on its owner's hand, which was protected by a big, leather gauntlet. The bird would be on a leash to stop it flying away and wearing a leather hood over its eyes, to stop the bird being distracted until the right moment. When the hood was removed and the leash released, the bird would fly up into the sky and then drop down on its prey below (a smaller bird) before returning to its master or mistress's hand.

Although falconry no longer exists as a sport today, quite a few castles in Britain put on falconry displays (without the killing) as special events during the summer. This gives you a chance to see the loving care and skill of the falconry along with the beauty of the birds themselves, and a taste of medieval times.

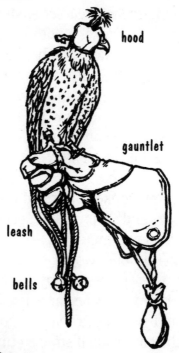

hood

gauntlet

leash

bells

purse (containing titbits as a reward)

Did you know?

One and a half million silver pennies were needed to pay the workers building Beaumaris Castle in North Wales their six months' wages. Paid for by the taxes collected by King Edward I, they had to be delivered in barrels!

Quick Quiz 8

1 How old were girls of noble blood when they were sent away to other castles?

2 Which English king had a chain of castles built in Wales?

3 What is a hennin?

4 What are illuminated manuscripts?

81 'Did castles really have torture chambers?'

I'm afraid so. The Middle Ages were pretty violent times and if a thumbscrew, hot pokers and, by the 14th century, a quick stretch on the rack made you give up a secret, confess or suffer, then your enemy might have been happy to try them on you.

82 'Could the rack really stretch you?'

Not like in the Laurel and Hardy film, where Hardy ends up walking around all long and thin after a few turns on the rack. It's the walking around part that's unlikely. A rack pulled its poor victim's arms in one direction and legs in the other, stretching muscles, sinews and bones and eventually breaking them.

83 'What's an iron maiden?'

From the outside, an iron maiden is a bit like a sarcophagus that mummified ancient Egyptians were buried in. It looks like an upright human-shaped coffin. When you open it, you'll find it has spikes on the inside walls and door. The victim was put inside and the door shut. Very painful.

84 'Where people really put in stocks?'

Yes. Unlike the nastier torture tools which were confined to the depths of the castle, stocks were fairly painless and could be found in towns and villages. The main idea was to humiliate the victim, who'd committed a far more minor offence. Sometimes they might just be laughed at. Other times, people might enjoy using them as target practice for their rotten vegetable throwing.

the stocks

85 'Did some dungeons flood at high tide?'

Yes. Some flooded by accident and some by design. With dungeons down in the depths of the castle (where light and heat wasn't considered important and security was high), they were often near the level of the moat, or river or sea. This meant they were often damp and, at high tide, very wet indeed. Some were, no doubt, deliberately designed to drown prisoners or, if not, give them a nasty fright if they were chained high up the wall. These were cruel and inhumane times.

86 'What's an oubliette?'

The kind of dungeon that, if you were put in it, you'd know it was very unlikely anyone was going to let you out alive. Oubliettes were often little more than a huge stone-lined hole in the ground with only one way in and out; the top through which you were dropped before the metal grill was put back in place. Sometimes they might remember to drop you food. Other times they might not. Prisoners in the oubliette were soon forgotten... in fact, the word comes from the French *oublier*, 'to forget'.

87 'Is it true that important prisoners weren't locked in the dungeon?'

It's absolutely true. If important people were captured on the battlefield, you treated them with great respect. Even though their movements would be under the watchful eye of the castle constable – who'd also be on the lookout for any spies trying to come in to communicate with them – an enemy baron or knight would be given much better food and accommodation than your servants. Why? The reasons were twofold: firstly, you'd want to be treated that way if *you* were taken prisoner and, secondly, because you can hold the prisoner to ransom. Noblemen came from rich families who would pay to have their loved ones returned to them safe and sound. This is one of the reasons for coats of arms. (See the answer to Question 29.)

88 'Were enemies' heads really put on spikes on battlements?'

Yes, this was common practice throughout Europe and wasn't just confined to castles. Executed villains or enemies often had their heads paraded on the battlements of walled towns, as a warning to others. Probably the most famous impaler of heads – sticker of heads onto spikes – was Vlad the Impaler, who was also known as Vlad Dracula... His name was later given to the world's most famous vampire!

89 'Who were the fighting monks?'

They were knights who were also monks... or monks who were also knights. For example, a group of them called the Knights Hospitaller cared for the sick and a group called the Knights Templar protected the Christian pilgrims visiting the Holy Land. When it came to the Crusades, though (see answer to Question 44) both the Hospitallers and the Templars fought against the Saracens.

Knights Hospitaller, red with a white cross

Knights Templar, white with a red cross

90 'What was the knight's vigil?'

If, after being trained as a pageboy and then as a squire, that squire is lucky enough to become a knight, there are certain rituals to be gone through. The evening before being dubbed a knight – and I'll come to that in a minute – he would have a bath and shave. And, yes, the bath would have been most unusual. He would then have been dressed (by fellow squires) in simple robes and taken to the chapel where he would pray ALL night. This was called the vigil.

The next morning, he'd dress in his very finest clothes and go to the great hall for a slap-up breakfast, after which he would be dubbed. Dubbing was when his lord, or even the king, touched his sword on the knight-to-be's shoulders. The man's whole family would be there and it was a very important occasion indeed. After being dubbed, the new knight would be presented with a sword of his own and a pair of spurs as symbols of his new power. (It's where the phrase 'earning your spurs' comes from.) Next, it would be back to the chapel for a blessing by the castle's priest, then off with his friends and family to celebrate on one of the proudest days of his life.

And, before anyone asks, yes, under certain circumstances, squires could be knighted on the battlefield. No time for the vigil then, just the dubbing (and, probably the promise of a sword and spurs later).

Quick Quiz 9

1 How did the oubliette get its name?

2 Who is Vlad the Impaler better known as?

3 What were the two main types of fighting monk?

91 'Why are some towers square and others round?'

Square towers are easier to build than round ones but not as strong. It is easier to cause the walls of a square tower to collapse by undermining (see the answer to Question 7) than it is a round one. The corners are most vulnerable to damage. Square rooms are, however, more convenient to furnish.

Round towers have two other main advantages. Firstly, a flat wall is easier for an enemy to climb than the rounded one. Secondly, on the battlements of a round tower you're standing in a circle with a 360 degrees field of vision and field of fire. There are no blind spots.

The solution? To have a big square keep (the big main inner tower where people lived), protected by an outer wall with plenty of round towers in it. By the time Henry VIII feared a French invasion, castles had gone through a radical redesign and there are some fine examples of castles with barely one straight wall between them.

92 'Why did some castles have really small outer walls that look easy to climb?'

Small is a relative term, but I know what you mean. Some castles' outer walls do seem strangely low, but there's a very good reason for it. Castles built this way, with a high inner wall with corner towers and excellent defences but with this much lower outer wall, are called concentric castles. The idea was that both inner and outer walls were heavily defended and that the soldiers on the higher, inner wall could fire over the heads of their comrades firing from the lower wall onto the attacking enemy. So the enemy was being attacked from different angles without the danger of the castle defenders shooting each other by mistake. If, however, the enemy breached (got over/through) the outer wall, it was easy for the defenders on the higher, inner wall to fire down on them. Concentric castles were a very clever piece of design. (See *The Changing Shape of Castles*, page 116.)

93 'Some pictures show wooden buildings a bit like long thin sheds on top of the ramparts. What were they?'

When the first stone castles were built they had

battlements at the top of towers and that was it. If you wanted to see what the enemy was up to directly below, you had to lean over the top, which made you an easy target. One quick lean and you could end up with a well-aimed enemy arrow in you. If you were leaning over to drop something on the enemy, you were even more of a target. The solution was bratting, the wooden overhangs you're talking about. Jutting out beyond the wall, and covered with a roof and wooden walls, you could lean over for a look through gaps in the bottom in relative safety. Bratting was no longer necessary when castles were built with machicolations (see the answer to Question 32), stone overhangs at the tops of towers with openings to look down and drop things through. Even castles with machicolations sometimes had wooden platforms added to the battlements for this purpose in times of war. These platforms were called hourds.

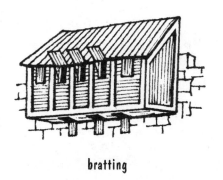

bratting

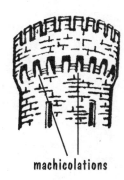

machicolations

94 'Did some castles really have windmills inside their walls?'

Yes but, to be more accurate, *on* their walls. A windmill in a courtyard wouldn't be much good. The walls would protect it from some of the wind. A wooden windmill would, therefore, be erected on top of a tower. These weren't a common sight, though. It was much more usual for corn to be ground in a windmill in the local village.

95 'What's a solar? A sauna?'

I often get asked about solars because they sound like they're something to do with the sun, as in 'solar energy'. In fact, the solar would be one of the finest rooms in the castle, used by the lord and lady as their private sitting room. In smaller castles, the bed chamber and solar were sometimes one and the same, but solars became bigger and grander as castles became bigger and grander. The solar was often on the same floor as the great hall, with an entrance near the high table. The time came when the lord and lady had a whole suite of rooms: the wardrobe, master bedroom, the solar and sometimes a basement containing their valuables.

96 'Was a wardrobe a room?'

Yes, the 'robe' refers to clothes and the 'ward'

refers to protecting (as in 'warding off evil spirits') but, instead of being a large cupboard as we know it today, a lord and lady's wardrobe was indeed a whole room. It wasn't just used to store clothes, though. Bed linen would have been stored here too, and some of the ladies' ladies-in-waiting may even have slept in here too. They might also have done sewing in here, and taught girls about household management. (See the answer to Question 79.)

97 'What happened during a typical day in a castle?'

It depended who you were and whether it was peacetime or war. In peacetime, if you're the kennel boy you might be exercising the dogs. If you're the falconer you're training the birds. If you're the farrier you're looking after the horses... the armourer is making and repairing weapons... the servants are going about their many, varied duties, the pages are training to be squires, the squires are training to be knights and the knights might be preparing for a joust. The lady of the house could be discussing an upcoming banquet with the chief steward whilst the constable is at the gate looking out for shifty strangers and the marshal is preparing the jousting field. The lord's treasurer may be counting the money from the lord's estates, protected by the sergeant at arms, whilst a gardener weeds the physic garden (full of herbs used by the apothecary who is busy mixing up a prescription) and the brewer makes beer of different strengths using water from the castle well. The priest is conducting prayers in the chapel, while the lord is being dressed in his greatest finery to meet a royal guest... If it's war, then everyone is geared up to defend the castle. The local villagers swell the number of inhabitants as they, and their livestock, seek safety within the walls. The male villagers will be put to work, acting as extra pairs of hands to carry rocks and weapons, and as extra pairs of eyes as lookouts. All guards are on duty, manning the towers and ramparts. Life is very different indeed. In other words, this question is near-impossible to answer!

98 'What question would you like to have been asked?'

One where I could really stress, once again, the importance of religion in everyday life in castles and in the code of the behaviour of knights: chivalry. There weren't just prayers before meals and prayers before battles but also the belief that true knights were fighting for good and for God. Chivalry was about doing-the-right-thing. The word 'generous' – meaning 'giving and open-handed' – originally meant well-born; in other words 'noble'. If you were noble, however, you were expected to care for those less well off than yourself, which is how the meaning of the word came to change. The word 'largess' literally means giving some of your largeness! In other words, using your importance (if you're a knight or Mr Big) to help others. Feudalism may seem an unfair system – and I certainly wouldn't have wanted to be a serf! – but not all masters were cruel and peasants were protected by their lords' castles too!

99 'How come you know so much about castles?'

Because all the evidence is there. Buildings and archaeology are our primary sources when studying life in the time of castles. We're very lucky because so many different types of castle have been built and remain. We can actually find out about castles by going to look at them.

Then there are the written primary sources. (Primary means that they were written, first hand, at the time rather than being retellings, second-hand information.) Primary written sources include letters, books and, just as importantly, words carved into walls and monuments. Writing on a nobleman's tomb could be full of useful information from the battles he fought in and who was his wife to which castle they lived in.

And then there's art and illustration (in illuminated manuscripts) of the time. A medieval tapestry might show a hunting scene, giving important information as to the weapons they used and the animals they hunted.

Then there are all the secondary sources: books, papers and articles written by scholars, historians and enthusiastic amateurs ever since. But people are still making new discoveries and finding out that little bit more all the time.

A beautifully illustrated letter from an illuminated manuscript

100 'Which are your favourite castles in Britain?'

My favourite castle in England to give visitors an idea of what life in medieval times was like is Warwick Castle in Warwickshire. Not only are there fabulous reconstructions, including waxwork models of people at work and play, but most summers, the castle grounds are filled with people in costumes playing the roles of everyone from knights and bowmen to jesters and potters. It's fun and informative.

My favourite castle in Scotland is Edinburgh Castle – not necessarily for the building itself but for its stunning location on top of a huge rocky outcrop, towering above the town.

And Wales? There are so many to choose from, but Beaumaris on the Isle of Anglesey comes out tops for me. It's certainly not the grandest, but it's a wonderful example of a concentric castle, and is very special.

But my favourite castle in *all* of Britain is on the Sussex/Kent border. It's called Bodiam and is surrounded by a perfect moat, fed by springs. From the outside it looks huge and whole. Inside, it is surprisingly small and a ruin.

The rear of Bodiam Castle

These are just my personal opinions. In Britain, we're spoilt for choice and, anyway, I reckon just about any castle anywhere in the world is worth a visit. (Check out *Famous Castles of the World*, starting on page 120).

100½ Why are castles castle-shaped?

The reason why I count this as half a question is because there's really no need for me to answer it. The answer lies in all the information about castles given in the earlier answers. In other words, much of the book explains why castles are castle-shaped... which is why I chose to name the book after this question. It's such a nice one! First and foremost, castles are about defence and it's these defence features – changing over time – which gave them their distinctive shape. You're very unlikely to find a castle with thin low walls and huge windows! You can read about *The Changing Shape of Castles* in the reference section, starting over the page...

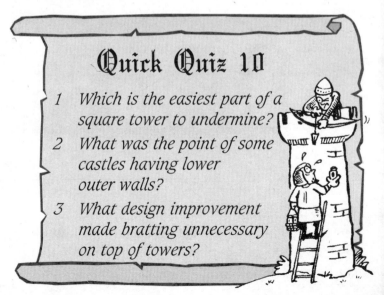

Quick Quiz 10

1 *Which is the easiest part of a square tower to undermine?*

2 *What was the point of some castles having lower outer walls?*

3 *What design improvement made bratting unnecessary on top of towers?*

THE CHANGING SHAPE OF CASTLES

Castle design changed over time. Some castles were adapted to incorporate the latest changes, others were built or rebuilt from scratch. Changes came in at different times in different parts of the world. Here are some of the most common basic designs in England and Wales, in the order in which they were first built.

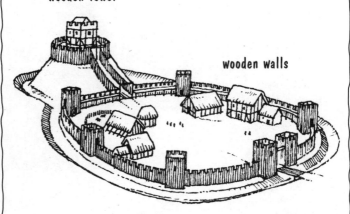

wooden tower

wooden walls

11th century motte and bailey

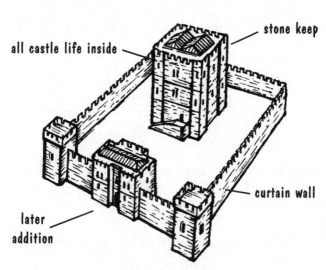

stone keep

all castle life inside

curtain wall

later
addition

12th century stone keep

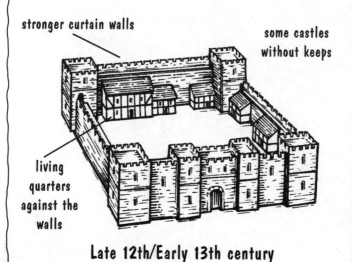

stronger curtain walls

some castles
without keeps

living
quarters
against the
walls

Late 12th/Early 13th century

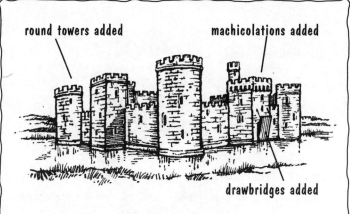

round towers added

machicolations added

drawbridges added

13th century castle
designers concentrated on adding defences to
existing castles

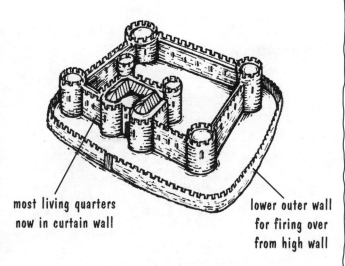

most living quarters
now in curtain wall

lower outer wall
for firing over
from high wall

Late 13th/Early 14th concentric castle

Although it has battlements, this is more of a manor house than castle. It is built for comfort, not defence

no real fortifications

big windows

14th century

Very thick rounded walls
(to resist cannon fire)

heavily defended with
guns, inside and out

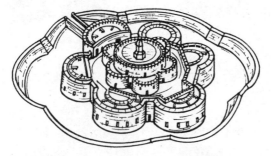

Mid 14th/Mid 16th century
with the fear of French invasion, the
last true castles were built on south east coast

FAMOUS CASTLES
OF THE WORLD

Castles in different parts of the world each have their own distinctive style. Here are just a few of the most famous, which best reflect the style of their country.

Himeji Castle, Japan built 1609

El Real de Manzanares, Spain, built 1475-80 in the Moorish style

Braubach Castle, Germany built in Middle Ages

Krak des Chevaliers, Syria
built in 12th century by warrior monks

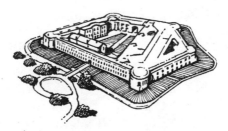

Fort Delaware, USA
built 1859 as a fortress but became a prison

The Kremlin, Russia
once a 12th century
city fortress

Glossary

arrow loops holes in castle walls through which arrows can be fired

bailey fenced area below a motte. (See *motte*)

banquet a large feast with many courses

battering ram a large beam of wood (later on wheels) designed to batter down wooden gates

battlements the parapets on top of castle walls, made of upright merlons and crenels (gaps) in-between

besiege to lay siege to a castle. (See *siege*)

bolt a crossbow arrow

concentric castles castles with two rings of defence: a high inner and lower outer wall. Those from the high inner wall could fire over the heads of those on the lower, outer one

Crusades holy wars in the Holy Land from 1096 to 1291

curfew an order to put out your fire and remain inside your town (or even inside your house) at night

falconry rearing and training birds of prey to hunt other birds for nobles' sport. (See *hawking*)

farrier a person who looked after horses

feudalism or **feudal system** the system of ruling by which land (and the serfs working on it) is awarded in return for loyalty

garderobe a castle loo

garrison troops stationed at a castle

gatehouse the entrance to the castle, usually heavily guarded

great hall the biggest room in the castle for banquets, important meetings and for the servants to sleep in

hawking hunting with birds of prey. (See *falconry*)

heraldry the study of coats of arms

high table 'top' table, the most important table in the great hall (usually on a platform)

hourds wooden structures placed on battlements, later replaced by machicolations

joust a contest at a tournament where one knight tries to knock another off his horse, using a lance

keep the main tower in the centre of a castle, containing living quarters

knight a highly trained noble warrior on horseback, called 'Sir', once a squire and before that a page

lance a very long spear-like weapon, used by knights in jousts

longbow a traditional bow and arrow, made of yew, and very large. (Up to 1.8 metres tall)

mace a weapon made up of a spiked metal ball on a small chain attached to a handle

machicolations overhanging battlements, allowing the dropping of objects, through holes, on people below

mantlet a wooden screen for attacking archers to hide behind, on the ground

mews wooden sheds used for housing falcons for falconry and hawking

moat a deep ditch surrounding many castles, usually full of water

motte a small man-made hill, with a basic castle on top. (See *bailey*)

murder holes holes in the ceiling of gatehouses, etc., through which everything from rocks to – yes! – boiling oil could be dropped on unwelcome visitors

oubliette a dungeon with one way in and one way out: through a hole in the top. People were often left to die in there. From French *oublier* meaning 'to forget'

page or **pageboy** a boy of noble blood training to be a squire, in the hope of becoming a knight. (See *squire* and *knight*)

portcullis a thick grill or grating which could be lowered to seal off a castle's gateway

quintain a 'target post' used by pages, squires and knights practising jousting. If hit off-centre, a weight could swing around and hit them

siege a blockade of a castle, stopping anyone or anything getting in or out (in the hope of forcing them to surrender). (See *besiege*)

solar the lord and lady's biggest, finest room in their apartments

spurs metal points fixed to a rider's boot heels to prick his horse's side to make it go faster. A symbol of knighthood

squire a former page training to be a knight. (See *page* and *knight*)

trebuchet a type of giant catapult for firing boulders at castle walls

trencher a thick slice of stale bread used as a plate and later given to the poor

undermining digging under the walls of a castle in the hope they'll collapse. Made impossible by moats, which would flood the tunnel

Quick Quiz Answers

Quick Quiz 1

1 Freemasons carved the stone
2 A farrier
3 Geologically impossible (too hard to dig or water drains away), no water supply, not thought necessary. Take your pick!
4 A barrack of soldiers
5 Woven twigs between timber, to make up a wall with daub

Quick Quiz 2

1 Arrow loops
2 A longbow arrow.
3 An ornament (often a bit like a sprout!) on top of an arch
4 Norman arches are rounded, gothic arches are pointed

Quick Quiz 3

1 To be born a boy with noble blood
2 Two
3 (b) and (c)

Quick Quiz 4

1 A licence to crenelate
2 So enemies on the bridge were easy targets for bowmen on the battlements
3 Another name for a siege tower (as well as being a bell tower in a church, for example)
4 The bombard

Quick Quiz 5

1 Garderobes
2 In the Holy Land (now Israel and Israeli-occupied territories)
3 Early chemists

Quick Quiz 6

1 A thick slice of stale bread, used as a plate
2 On a spit in front of an open fire
3 Their daggers
4 The trenchers were given to the poor, and much of the rest was thrown to the dogs

Quick Quiz 7

1 The correct term for a suit of armour
2 The code of conduct knights were supposed to live by, to make them 'good'
3 By linking tiny loops of metal

Quick Quiz 8

1 About six years old
2 Edward I
3 A tall, pointed hat
4 Handwritten, highly decorated books and documents (often with pictures within the larger letters)

Quick Quiz 9

1 It comes from the french for *oublier*, 'to forget'
2 Dracula
3 Knights Hospitallers and Knights Templars

Quick Quiz 10

1 The corners
2 So the attackers can be fired on from two angles
3 Machicolations

INDEX